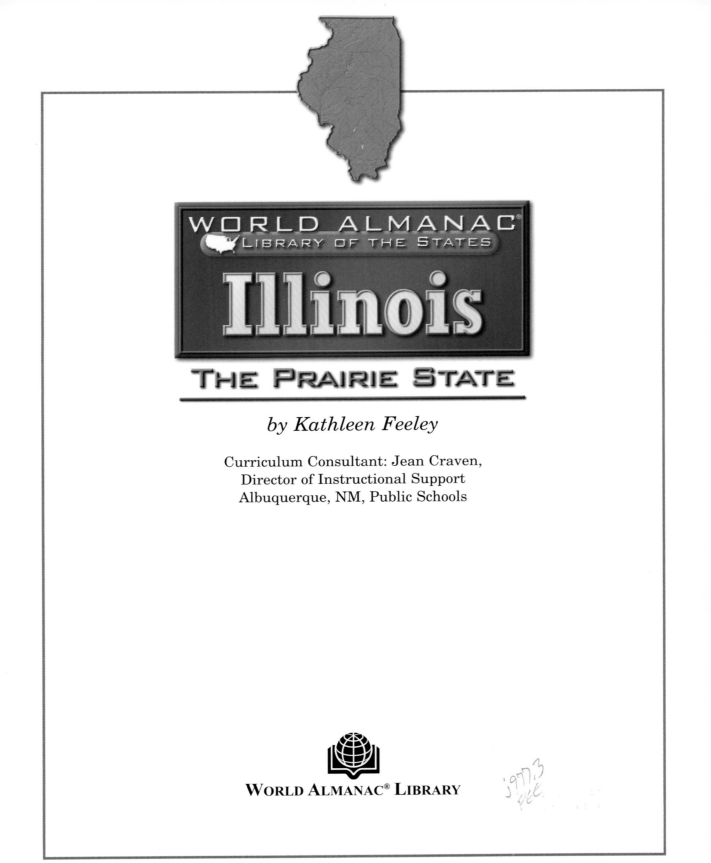

WORLD ALMANAC® LIBRARY OF THE STATES

Illinois

THE PRAIRIE STATE

by Kathleen Feeley

Curriculum Consultant: Jean Craven,
Director of Instructional Support
Albuquerque, NM, Public Schools

WORLD ALMANAC® LIBRARY

Please visit our web site at: www.worldalmanaclibrary.com
For a free color catalog describing World Almanac® Library's list of high-quality books
and multimedia programs, call 1-800-848-2928 or fax your request to (414) 332-3567.

Library of Congress Cataloging-in-Publication Data

Feeley, Kathleen, 1968-
   Illinois, the Prairie State / by Kathleen Feeley.
      p. cm. — (World Almanac Library of the states)
   Includes bibliographical references and index.
   Summary: Illustrations and text present the history, geography, people, politics and
government, economy, and social life and customs of Illinois.
   ISBN 0-8368-5115-3 (lib. bdg.)
   ISBN 0-8368-5284-2 (softcover)
   1. Illinois—Juvenile literature. [1. Illinois.] I. Title. II. Series.
F541.3.F44   2002
977.3—dc21   2001046990

This edition first published in 2002 by
World Almanac® Library
330 West Olive Street, Suite 100
Milwaukee, WI 53212 USA

This edition © 2002 by World Almanac® Library.

Design and Editorial: **Jack&Bill**/Bill SMITH STUDIO Inc.
Editors: Jackie Ball and Kristen Behrens
Art Directors: Ron Leighton and Jeffrey Rutzky
Photo Research and Buying: Christie Silver and Sean Livingstone
Design and Production: Maureen O'Connor and Jeffrey Rutzky
World Almanac® Library Editors: Patricia Lantier, Amy Stone, Valerie J. Weber,
Catherine Gardner, Carolyn Kott Washburne, Alan Wachtel, Monica Rausch
World Almanac® Library Production: Scott M. Krall, Eva Erato-Rudek, Tammy Gruenewald

Photo credits: p. 6 (all) © Corel; p. 7 (top) © Sandy Felsenthal/CORBIS; (bottom) © Library of
Congress; p. 9 (top) © Dover Publications, (bottom) © Michael S. Lewis/CORBIS; p. 10
© Univ. of Chicago Library Special Collections; p. 11 © ArtToday; p. 12 © Library of Congress;
p. 13 © Advertising Ephemera Collection/Duke University Special Collections Library; p. 14
© Library of Congress; p. 15 (top) © Terry Ashe/TimePix; p. 17 courtesy of Illinois Bureau of
Tourism; p. 18 © Steve Liss/TimePix; p. 19 courtesy of Illinois Bureau of Tourism; p. 20 (all)
courtesy of Illinois Bureau of Tourism; p. 21 (from left to right) courtesy of Illinois Bureau of
Tourism, courtesy of Springfield CVB, courtesy of Illinois Bureau of Tourism; p. 26 (from left to
right) © PhotoDisc, © Painet; p. 27 © Corel; p. 29 courtesy of Illinois Board of Tourism;
p. 30 courtesy of Illinois General Assembly; p. 31–33 (all) © Library of Congress; p. 34 (from left
to right) © Jeffrey Rutzky, courtesy of Springfield CVB; p. 35 © Tom G. Lynn/TimePix; p. 36 (from
left to right) © Corel, © Jeffrey Rutzky, p. 37 courtesy of Illinois Bureau of Tourism; p. 39
(clockwise) © PhotoDisc, © Alfred Eisenstaedt/TimePix, © Leonard McCombe/TimePix; p. 40
© Artville; p. 41 (top) © Artville, (bottom) © John W McDonough/TimePix; p. 42–43 © Library of
Congress; p. 44 (all) © PhotoDisc; p. 45 (top) © PhotoDisc, (bottom)

Printed in the United States of America

1 2 3 4 5 6 7 8 9 06 05 04 03 02

Illinois

Hub of the Nation

The pioneering spirit transformed the Illinois landscape from prairie land to a patchwork of farms and cities. This same spirit transformed the agricultural nature of Illinois' economy in the early nineteenth century to one that's vibrant and diverse — and the fourth-largest in the United States.

Chicago, the state's economic capital if not the seat of its government, is home to the second-largest financial market in the country after New York City. Chicago also processes many of the state's agricultural products and is one of the largest meat markets in the world. The city occupies this central position in the economy because it is a national transportation hub for railroads and airways. Waterways, too, are spokes in the network — Chicago's ports on Lake Michigan provide access to the St. Lawrence Seaway and the Atlantic Ocean.

Chicago's contributions in people and achievements to the nation's cultural heritage have been immense and wide-ranging. Innovative Chicago musicians helped create jazz in its many forms, and the Art Institute of Chicago showcases one of the country's most important collections of modern art.

Chicago and much of the rest of the state have even more than the accomplishments of talented individuals; there is an overall spirit — a social consciousness and commitment to progressive politics. The state, known as the Land of Lincoln, embodies a progressive spirit not only found in his legacy but also in the pioneering work of social reformer Jane Addams, among others. Forward-thinking and rich in physical and cultural resources, Illinois has thrived as the hub of a busy nation.

▶ Map of Illinois showing state highway system, as well as major cities and waterways.

▼ Map of downtown Chicago.

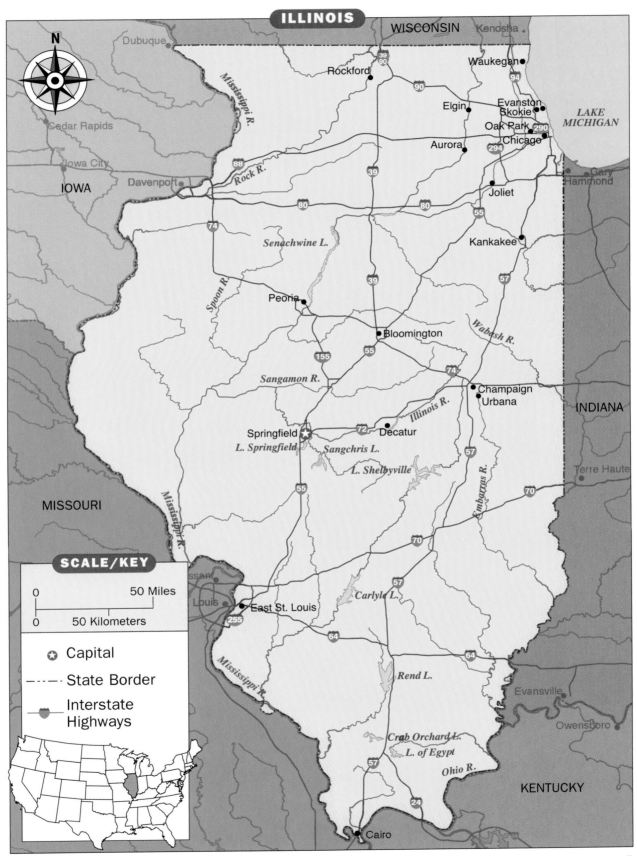

WISCONSIN
Kenosha

Dubuque

N

Rockford

Waukegan

94

Elgin
Evanston
Skokie

90

39
90

Cedar Rapids

LAKE
MICHIGAN

Oak Park
290
Chicago

Aurora
294

Mississippi R.

88

Rock R.

39

Iowa City

IOWA

Davenport

80

80

Joliet

Gary
Hammond

55

74

Senachwine L.

Kankakee

57

Spoon R.

39

Peoria

Wabash R.

Bloomington

155

55

Sangamon R.

Illinois R.

74

Champaign
Urbana

INDIANA

Springfield
L. Springfield

72

Decatur

Sangchris L.

L. Shelbyville

57

Embarras R.

Terre Haute

55

70

MISSOURI

Mississippi R.

70

SCALE/KEY

0   50 Miles

0   50 Kilometers

57

Carlyle L.

Louis

255

East St. Louis

64

64

Capital

State Border

Interstate
Highways

Mississippi R.

Rend L.

Evansville

Owensboro

Crab Orchard L.
L. of Egypt

57

Ohio R.

24

KENTUCKY

Cairo

Fast Facts

ILLINOIS

ILLINOIS (IL), The Prairie State

Entered Union

December 3, 1818 (21st state)

Capital — **Population**

Springfield 111,454

Total Population (2000)

12,419,293 (5th most populous state)

Largest Cities — **Population**

Chicago 2,896,016
Rockford 150,115
Aurora 142,990
Naperville 128,358
Peoria 112,936

Land Area

55,584 square miles (143,963 square kilometers) (24th largest state)

State Motto

"State Sovereignty, National Union"

State Song

"Illinois" *by Charles Chamberlin and Archibald Johnston*

State Bird

Cardinal — *The male cardinal is easily spotted because of his bright red plumage.*

State Game Animal

White-tailed Deer — *The schoolchildren of Illinois voted to make the deer the state animal in 1980.*

State Fish

Bluegill — *Noted for being one of the best fighting game fish, the bluegill grows to about 9 inches (23 centimeters) and weighs less then 1 pound (454 grams).*

State Insect

Monarch Butterfly — *A third-grader from Decatur suggested making the Monarch Illinois's state insect in 1974.*

State Tree

White Oak — *Illinois's official tree was originally the Native Oak and was changed in 1973 to the White Oak.*

State Flower

Native Violet — *This small, purplish blossom grows naturally throughout Illinois.*

State Mineral

Fluorite — *Illinois is the largest producer of fluorite in the United States. Steel, enamels, aluminum, glass, and many chemicals are produced with the help of fluorite.*

State Fossil

Tully Monster — *A soft-bodied marine animal, the Tully Monster lived 280 to 340 million years ago. More than one hundred Tully Monster fossils have been discovered only in Illinois.*

State Dance

Square Dance — *Square dancing was a popular social activity during Illinois's pioneer days in the 1800s.*

PLACES TO VISIT

Abraham Lincoln's Home and Burial Site, *Springfield*

Visitors can see the one-and-a-half-story cottage that Lincoln and his wife lived in until he became president in 1860. The cottage is situated within a four-block historic neighborhood.

Museum of Science and Industry, *Chicago*

This attraction includes many hands-on exhibits, including the world's largest model train display, the *Apollo 8* command module, and an airplane exhibit. Temporary shows highlight the latest issues and advances in science.

Cahokia Mounds State Historic Site, *Collinsville*

Ruins of a once-bustling Middle Mississippi city, inhabited from about A.D. 900 to 1500, have been carefully preserved, along with many of the earthen mounds the Native Americans built for religious and burial purposes.

For other places and events to attend, see p. 44.

BIGGEST, BEST, AND MOST

- The Sears Tower in Chicago, completed in 1974, is the tallest building in North America.
- Chicago O'Hare is one of the world's busiest airports.

STATE FIRSTS

- 1885 — The world's first skyscraper, the Home Insurance Building, was completed in downtown Chicago.
- 1920 — Illinois was the first state to ratify the 19th Amendment, giving women the right to vote.
- 1978 — Hannah Gray became president of University of Chicago, the first woman president of a major U.S. university.
- 1992 — Carol Moseley-Braun was elected to the U.S. Senate in 1992, the first African-American woman senator.

Burger Flipping 101?

Illinois is home to an institution called Hamburger University. Founded in 1961 in Oak Brook, Hamburger University is the official management training center for the McDonald's corporation. Aspiring restaurant managers can attend to learn the basics of McDonald's operations, as well as how to manage their own McDonald's franchise. To date more than seventy thousand people have "graduated" from Hamburger University, which includes a staff of about thirty qualified "professors."

Windy City, Wisconsin?

When Europeans first came to Lake Michigan, Chicago was an Indian village.

Settlers had established a small town there by the time Illinois became an American territory. When Congress was in the process of making Illinois a state, they had its northern border running west from the southern tip of Lake Michigan. If it hadn't been for a territorial delegate named Nathaniel Pope, who argued for moving the border 40 miles (64 km) to the north, Chicago would have ended up as a Wisconsin city.

The Crossroads State

A house divided against itself cannot stand. I believe this government cannot endure permanently half slave and half free.

— *Abraham Lincoln, 1858*

The first inhabitants of Illinois were nomadic hunters who came to the region about ten thousand years ago. Their descendants, the Middle Mississippi Indians, formed a complex culture and cultivated corn, squash, and other crops. They built vast cities organized around a central plaza, consisting of large earth mounds used for religious and burial purposes. One of the largest, Monk's Mound, near Cahokia, Illinois, still stands. A major religious center, it stretches 1,000 feet (304 meters) long, more than 700 feet (213 m) wide, and 100 feet (30 m) tall. The Middle Mississippi culture was disappearing, probably due to disease and overpopulation, by the time the first Europeans began to explore North America.

When Europeans first arrived in Illinois, they encountered a confederation of tribes, including the Kaskaskia, Peoria, and Tamaroa, that spoke the Algonquian language. These tribes hunted bison and deer and grew corn and other vegetables.

Native Americans of Illinois
Cahokia
Fox
Kaskaskia
Michigamea
Peoria
Sauk
Tamaroa

Exploration and Conflict

The French were the first Europeans to explore and settle in Illinois. A French expedition to explore the Mississippi River, led by explorer and mapmaker Louis Jolliet and Jesuit missionary priest Jacques Marquette, reached the area in 1673. Two years later Marquette founded a mission near present-day Utica. French explorer Robert LaSalle, on an expedition to find the mouth of the Mississippi River, established Fort Crevecoeur in 1680 near present-day Peoria.

While the French claimed possession of Illinois, the permanent settlements they established were mainly Jesuit missions and forts for fur trading. After the French and

DID YOU KNOW?

The name *Illinois* comes from the Algonquian word *Illiniwek,* meaning "the men."

Indian War (1754–1763), the French turned over most of their territory in North America, including Illinois, to the British. But France's Native American allies did not accept British control. To reduce conflict between European settlers and Indians, British leaders issued the Proclamation Line of 1763, banning white settlement west of the Appalachian Mountains, an area that included Illinois. But many British colonists ignored this proclamation and moved west to settle in Illinois territory.

The colonists rebelled against Britain during the Revolutionary War (1776–1783). Patriot leader George Rogers Clark came to Illinois in 1778 with a small band of Continental troops. They captured the British-controlled settlements of Kaskaskia and Cahokia on the Mississippi River, gaining Illinois for the rebelling colonists. Illinois was made a colony of Virginia until after the war, when Virginia turned the territory over to the new United States government.

◀ **Patriot leader George Rogers Clark.**

DID YOU KNOW?

When the British took control of Illinois in 1763, many French settlers left Illinois and moved to Spanish-controlled areas west of the Mississippi River because they did not want to live under British rule.

▼ **Burial mounds of a Native American civilization that existed in the Cahokia Mounds State Historic Site area from A.D. 900 to 1500.**

From Territory to State

After the Revolutionary War the new U.S. government was in debt. To raise funds, the government decided to sell the land in the Northwest Territory, which included Illinois. Congress passed the 1784, 1785, and 1787 Northwest Ordinances, explaining how Illinois would be settled to become a state. Settlers could buy land at one dollar per acre as long as they purchased a minimum of one square mile (640 acres or 259 hectares). Slavery was banned, and settlers were given a bill of rights to ensure their freedom. Before Illinois became a state on December 3, 1818, a deal was made to re-draw the boundaries of Illinois to include the small port city of Chicago.

The Mormons

In 1830 Joseph Smith, a New York State farmer, founded the Church of Jesus Christ of Latter-day Saints. Smith and his followers, known as Mormons, were persecuted for their beliefs and left New York to find religious freedom farther west. In 1839 the Mormons arrived in Commerce, Illinois, where they built a city and religious center named Nauvoo. This Mormon community prospered, and the population

DID YOU KNOW?

According to legend, Mrs. Kate O'Leary's cow knocked over a lantern in a barn, starting the Great Chicago Fire of 1871.

▼ Joseph Smith, who founded the Church of Jesus Christ of Latter-day Saints, lived in this house in Nauvoo, Illinois.

quickly reached more than twenty thousand residents. Tensions between Mormons and non-Mormons continued, and in July 1844 Joseph Smith was arrested and jailed in Carthage, Illinois, where he was killed by an anti-Mormon mob. Smith's followers, now under the leadership of Brigham Young, left Nauvoo in 1846 and resettled in Salt Lake City, Utah.

Land of Lincoln

Abraham Lincoln moved to Illinois in 1830 at the age of twenty-one. Like many settlers in Illinois, Lincoln and his family came to Illinois to make a better life. Lincoln worked at many jobs — rail splitter, storekeeper, surveyor — before enlisting in the Illinois militia.

In 1832 Native American leader Black Hawk led a group of Sauk and Fox Indians against white settlers along the Rock River in Illinois. He brought in a party of about one thousand men, women, and children to reclaim the land. The Illinois militia was called in to drive out the Indians, with Abraham Lincoln serving as captain of his militia company. Black Hawk was quickly subdued, and as a condition of their surrender, the Indians were forced to give up their claims on all land in Illinois and to move farther west.

After the war Lincoln served in the Illinois state legislature from 1835 to 1841. He began to practice law in 1836 and moved to Springfield, the new capital of Illinois, in 1837. He entered national politics in 1846, when he was elected to the U.S. House of Representatives, where he served one term. When he challenged Stephen Douglas for his U.S. Senate seat in 1858, the two politicians engaged in a series of famous debates about slavery and American society. Although Lincoln lost the Senate election to Douglas, the debates earned him national prominence, and two years later he was elected president.

With Lincoln's election South Carolina withdrew from the Union, and other Southern

Black Hawk
1767–1838

Sauk and Fox tribal land in Illinois was turned over to the U.S. government in 1804. Many Native Americans, including the Sauk warrior Black Hawk (his Sauk name was Ma-ka-tai-me-she-kia-kiak), became hostile to the United States. Black Hawk, and many others, fought on the British side during the War of 1812. The number of white settlements continued to increase in the 1820s and 1830s, and tensions grew as well. Black Hawk became the leader of a group of Sauk and Fox who were determined to reclaim their homelands. In defiance of orders from the U.S. federal government that relocated the Sauk and Fox west of the Mississippi, Black Hawk continued to lead parties back to their villages in Illinois. Finally, in April 1832, the Illinois militia and U.S. troops were called out to expel the group of Native men, women, and children. The fighting lasted about three months, and in the end most of Black Hawk's warriors had been killed. After the Black Hawk War, the Sauk and Fox gave up all claims to land in Illinois and retreated west. Black Hawk was imprisoned, paraded around cities on the East Coast as an Indian warrior, and returned to the Sauk, where he wrote his life story in 1833 and died in 1838.

states followed. The Civil War began in 1861, with Illinois on the side of the Union. Approximately 250,000 Illinois men fought for the Union cause during the Civil War. Under Lincoln's leadership, the Union defeated the South after four years of bloody conflict. On April 14, 1865, just days after the Civil War ended, Lincoln was assassinated.

Chicago and the Transportation Revolution

Chicago was a small settlement on the shores of Lake Michigan until the 1830s, when the transportation revolution transformed it into a center for trade and industry. The Erie Canal opened in upstate New York in 1825, linking the Great Lakes to the Hudson River and New York Harbor. This opened a major route for transportation and trade between the Midwest and New York City, sparking the rapid growth of Chicago. In 1848 the Illinois & Michigan Canal was completed to connect the Great Lakes to the Mississippi River. That same year the Chicago Board of Trade was established. This organization standardized the grain market and set prices for the large volume of farm commodities that arrived in Chicago from the rich farmlands of southern Illinois and the rest of the Midwest.

Railroads quickly replaced canals as the best way to transport goods from the farms to the cities. Between 1850 and 1900 thousands of miles of railroad tracks were laid across the nation, and Illinois prospered from the railroad boom. In 1852, Chicago became the western terminus of two railroad lines from the eastern United States. By 1880 Chicago had more than twenty railroad lines running

▼ In 1907 the largest engine in the world belonged to the Chicago & Alton Railroad Company.

through it, connecting the city and all of Illinois with the rest of the United States and much of Canada. Other industries developed in Chicago as the city became the link between the industrial Northeast and the agricultural Midwest. These included mail-order retail businesses and department stores such as Sears Roebuck and Montgomery Ward, as well as meatpacking and the manufacture of metal products and railroad cars.

The Great Chicago Fire of 1871

It was the completeness of the wreck; the total desolation which met the eye on every hand; the utter blankness of what had a few hours before been so full of life, of associations, of aspirations, of all things which kept the mind of a Chicagoan so constantly driven.
— Elias Colbert and Everett Chamberlin, Chicago and the Great Conflagration, 1871.

On the evening of October 8, 1871, a fire started in downtown Chicago. It raged for two days, until rain helped put it out. When the fire was finally extinguished, Chicagoans took stock of the damage. The burned-out section of the city covered 4 square miles (10 sq km) and included the business district. More than ninety thousand residents were homeless, and about eighteen thousand buildings had been destroyed, totaling more than $2 million in property losses. Although the fire was devastating, only an estimated 250 people died, out of a population of 330,000.

Over the next two years, Chicago was rapidly rebuilt with the help of craftsmen and workers from all over the nation. These buildings were built to meet new fire safety regulations. In the 1880s the age of the modern steel-frame skyscraper was born in Chicago's business district. Steel frames allowed structures to stand much taller than had been possible with older construction methods. The first skyscraper was the Home Insurance Building in downtown Chicago, designed by William LeBaron Jenney and completed in 1885.

Mail Order

In August 1872 Aaron Montgomery Ward founded the first U.S. mail order business for general merchandise. Montgomery Ward and Company was headquartered in Chicago to take advantage of its vast transportation network, which enabled the company to send goods to customers throughout the nation. The business prospered, since it allowed people who lived in rural areas far from retail stores to purchase items they needed by mail. A major competitor appeared on the scene when the Sears Roebuck and Company mail order business relocated to Chicago in 1893. By 1895 the Sears catalog contained 532 pages of goods, from clothing to bedding to toys. Sears and Montgomery Ward opened their first retail stores in Chicago in the 1920s. These retail and catalog giants were very important to the Illinois economy. In 2001 Montgomery Ward closed its doors after 129 years of business, but its national headquarters in Chicago remains a national historic landmark. Sears remains in Chicago, a national retailer with a long history.

Workers Unite!

Illinois was the focus of much labor unrest during the end of the nineteenth century. In 1886 workers and union organizers gathered in Haymarket Square in Chicago to demand an eight-hour workday. The event turned violent, and several police and protesters were killed in the rioting. During a general railroad strike in 1894, workers participated throughout the nation, bringing rail traffic in Chicago and the rest of Illinois to a halt for two months. The strike sparked so many violent incidents and disrupted American business to such an extent that President Grover Cleveland called in federal troops to force the protesters back to work. Social activist Jane Addams, founder of Hull House in Chicago, was the leader in the workers' demand for shorter workdays. The efforts of Addams and other reformers did not finally pay off until 1938. In that year the eight-hour workday was established by the National Fair Labor Standards Act.

Twentieth Century

From 1917 to 1918 Illinois sent more than 300,000 men to Europe to fight in World War I. After the war the state benefited from the nationwide economic boom. Black Americans migrated to Chicago from the South in the thousands, seeking greater economic and social opportunities in this period of postwar prosperity. Illinois suffered with the rest of the nation when the Great Depression struck in 1929, bringing with it record unemployment and poverty. The discovery of oil in central and southern Illinois in 1939 helped improve the state's

....

▼ After the great fire of 1871, much of Chicago lay in ruins.

The Chicago School

In 1867 William LeBaron Jenney founded an architectural firm in Chicago that trained many important architects and played a central role in the development of the skyscraper. This group of architects, which included Louis Sullivan and Daniel H. Burnham, came to be known as the "Chicago School." Though some of their work has been demolished over the years — such as the Home Insurance Building — much of it remains today as historic landmarks. Some of their most important buildings are the Auditorium Theatre, home to dance and theater in Chicago today, and the Carson Pirie Scott and Company Building in downtown Chicago. Chicago is considered by many to be the home of modern architecture because of the influential work of these architects.

economy, but the nation didn't truly recover until war once again broke out in Europe.

Chicago played a key role during World War II, when scientists with the University of Chicago worked on the Manhattan Project, the top-secret federal program to develop the atomic bomb. In 1942, Enrico Fermi and a group of scientists created the world's first controlled atomic chain reaction in one of the university's laboratories.

Richard J. Daley served as mayor of Chicago from 1955 until his death in 1976. During his career Daley built a powerful Democratic base in the city and the state that came to have powerful influence nationwide. Some criticized him for having too much power, while others applauded his ability to get things done. Daley instituted major urban renewal in Chicago, transforming the business district once again and keeping the city prosperous as other American urban centers went into decline.

Illinois produced other prominent leaders, including Ronald Reagan, born in Tampico, Illinois. Reagan served two terms as the president of the United States, from 1980 to 1988. In 1992, Illinois voters elected Carol Moseley-Braun, the nation's first African-American woman senator. Throughout Illinois' history, its people have shown an innovative, determined spirit, one that has helped the state pull through in difficult times and contribute leaders and resources to the rest of the nation.

▲ Carol Moseley-Braun, Democratic senator from Illinois, was the first African-American woman ever elected to the U.S. Senate. Of the attention she received because of this, Moseley-Braun said, "All I really want to be is boring. When people talk about me, I'd like them to say: Carol's basically a short Bill Bradley. Or: Carol's kind of like Al Gore in a skirt."

Farmers and City Dwellers

> We struck the home trail now, and in a few hours were in that astounding Chicago — a city where they are always rubbing a lamp and fetching up a genii, and contriving and achieving new possibilities.
>
> — *Mark Twain*, Life on the Mississippi, *1883*

With more than 12.4 million people, Illinois is the fifth most populous state in the nation. It is a diverse mix of people. Many have emigrated from other countries or are descended from immigrants of earlier times. Forty-nine percent of the current population is male, while 51 percent is female. The median age in Illinois is 34.7 years, slightly older than the rest of the nation, where the median age is 32.8.

Education
Illinois has a very well-educated population. About 75 percent of adult Illinoisans have a high school diploma, and approximately 20 percent have graduated from college.

Age Distribution in Illinois	
0–4	876,549
5–19	2,728,957
20–34	2,662,517
35–54	3,610,612
55–64	1,040,633
65 & over	1,500,025

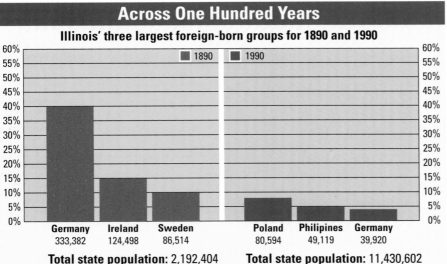

Across One Hundred Years
Illinois' three largest foreign-born groups for 1890 and 1990

■ 1890   ■ 1990

Germany	Ireland	Sweden	Poland	Philipines	Germany
333,382	124,498	86,514	80,594	49,119	39,920

Total state population: 2,192,404
Total foreign-born: 842,347 (38%)

Total state population: 11,430,602
Total foreign-born: 952,272 (8%)

Patterns of Immigration
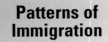
The total number of people who immigrated to Illinois in 1998 was 13,163. Of that number, the largest immigrant groups were from Mexico (30%), India (10%), and Poland (10%).

Immigration

Immigration has always played an important part in shaping the population, life, and culture in Illinois. After the French and Indian War, many of the French who had settled in Illinois moved elsewhere, not wishing to be under British control. At the same time settlers from the British

▲ The Chicago River flows through downtown Chicago.

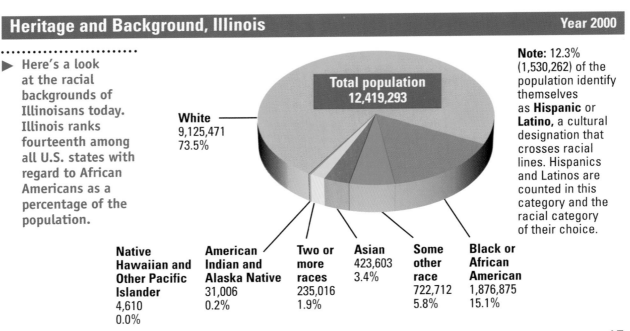

Heritage and Background, Illinois — Year 2000

► Here's a look at the racial backgrounds of Illinoisans today. Illinois ranks fourteenth among all U.S. states with regard to African Americans as a percentage of the population.

Total population 12,419,293

White
9,125,471
73.5%

Note: 12.3% (1,530,262) of the population identify themselves as **Hispanic** or **Latino,** a cultural designation that crosses racial lines. Hispanics and Latinos are counted in this category and the racial category of their choice.

Native Hawaiian and Other Pacific Islander
4,610
0.0%

American Indian and Alaska Native
31,006
0.2%

Two or more races
235,016
1.9%

Asian
423,603
3.4%

Some other race
722,712
5.8%

Black or African American
1,876,875
15.1%

Educational Levels of Illinois Workers	
Less than 9th grade	528,183
9th to 12th grade, no diploma	752,138
High school graduate, including equivalency	2,290,896
Some college, no degree	1,614,640
Associate degree	487,679
Bachelor's degree	1,328,906
Graduate or professional degree	771,427

colonies on the Atlantic coast moved west to Illinois. When the Irish and Germans emigrated to the United States in large numbers beginning in the 1840s, many settled in northern Illinois.

As successive waves of immigrants arrived in the United States from northern and then eastern and southern Europe in the late nineteenth and early twentieth centuries, many settled in Illinois, particularly in the urban centers. Industry and manufacturing in the cities attracted immigrants from all over with the promise of steady work.

▼ Sal Dimiceli, a Chicago businessman, founded The Time Is Now, a nonprofit organization that donates goods, services, and cash to the needy people of Pembroke township.

In 1910 the immigrants with the largest populations in Illinois were German, Austrian/Hungarian, Russian, Scandinavian, Irish, and Italian. Today immigration continues as people arrive in the state from all over the world. From 1980 to 1990 more than 370,000 immigrants moved to Illinois.

African Americans

Over 1.8 million African Americans live in Illinois today. The first arrivals were slaves who came with their owners in the 1700s. After Illinois became a state in 1818, slavery was banned (although slave owners were allowed to keep their slaves). African Americans at that time consisted of a mix of slaves and freedmen. The African-American population of Illinois grew steadily after the Civil War and the abolition of slavery. When the United States entered World War I in 1917, cities in the North suddenly had a high demand for workers. This situation set off the "Great Migration," in which hundreds of thousands of African Americans moved from the rural South to cities in the North. Black migration to Illinois skyrocketed, with a major destination being the high-paying wartime factories of Chicago. In 1910 the African-American population in Illinois was 109,000; by 1930, this figure had risen to over 1.1 million.

▲ Illinois is home to many varied communities, among them the Amish of Arcola. The Amish, one of the "plain sects," are mostly of German descent.

Religion

Nearly one quarter of Illinoisans belong to Catholic churches. Among the 38 percent of Illinoisans who are Protestant Christians, the largest percentage are Baptists. Other Protestant groups include Lutherans, Methodists, Presbyterians, and Episcopalians. Illinoisans who are Muslim make up 0.4 percent of the total state population; there are seventy-one mosques and Muslim community centers throughout the state. More than 250,000 Illinoisans are Jewish, served by 184 synagogues and temples.

Rural *vs.* Urban

The majority of Illinois's residents live either in a city, town, or suburb. Nearly three million people live in Chicago, and millions more live in its surrounding suburbs. An estimated 14 percent of the population lives in rural areas. About two hundred thousand of these rural inhabitants live and work on the farms in downstate Illinois.

The Long State

> A rolling plain spread before us, the farther side bounded
> by timber, while the prairie itself was free from tree
> or brush, except where some interesting stream was
> followed by a narrow line of thicket.
>
> — *Dr. R. Ridgeway, "The Ornithology of Illinois," 1913*

Although nicknamed the Prairie State, Illinois features a variety of landscapes and vegetation. And although it is firmly rooted in America's Midwest, Illinois benefits from access to several major waterways, linking it to the Atlantic Ocean and the Gulf of Mexico.

With a land area of 55,584 square miles (143,963 sq km), Illinois is the twenty-fourth largest state in the nation, falling in the middle of the fifty states. It occupies a central location on the continent as well. From Chicago, located on the shore of Lake Michigan, one can travel by water through the Great Lakes Huron, Erie, and Ontario, into the Saint Lawrence River, and out to the Atlantic Ocean. Chicago also has access to southern waterways — the Chicago River flows to the Mississippi River, which empties into the Gulf of Mexico.

North to south, the state stretches 385 miles (620 km), from Lake Michigan to the town of Cairo, where the Mississippi and Ohio Rivers converge.

DID YOU KNOW?

■Illinois's northern latitude matches that of Portsmouth, New Hampshire, and the state's southern latitude matches up with Portsmouth, Virginia.

High Point

Charles Mound
1,235 feet
(376 m)

▼ *From left to right:*
An eagle; downtown Chicago; prairie land; Illinois autumn; historic New Salem; Starved Rock State Park.

Ancient Rock, Rich Soil

During the last ice age, glaciers covered about 90 percent of Illinois. When they receded, they left behind layers of thick, black soil in the northern and central parts of the state that is among the most fertile in the world. Today these areas are part of the United States' agricultural heartland. The soil in the southern part of Illinois is thinner, less fertile, and less well suited to agriculture.

Topography

Flat prairies cover a large part of Illinois. Low rolling hills lie to the northwest, west, and south. The highest point in the state is in the northwest — Charles Mound is 1,235 feet (376 meters) high. The lowest point is 279 feet (85 m) at the Mississippi River.

To the south lie the gently sloping Shawnee Hills, which are covered with forest. They are the northern foothills of the Ozark Mountains. At the southern tip of the state, bordered by the Ohio and Mississippi Rivers, is the Shawnee National Forest.

Climate

Because of its geographic location and its long north–south axis, Illinois experiences large seasonal and regional variations in temperature and rainfall. The growing season varies from one hundred fifty-five days in the northernmost counties to two hundred-five days in the far south.

Cold, dry air masses from Canada collide with warm, moist air from the Gulf of Mexico, causing weather in Illinois to change quickly. Abrupt changes in temperature can occur within the space of a few hours. Violent thunderstorms, particularly in the spring, can breed killer tornadoes.

Situated on the coast of Lake Michigan, Chicago experiences dramatic weather as well. Its nickname, "the

DID YOU KNOW?

Until the nineteenth century the Chicago River flowed eastward into Lake Michigan. Then a series of locks was built to alter the direction of flow westward, so the river now empties into the Mississippi.

Average January temperature
Chicago: 22°F (-6°C)
Cairo: 37°F (3°C)

Average July temperature
Chicago: 74°F (23°C)
Cairo: 80°F (27°C)

Average yearly rainfall
Chicago: 34 inches (86 cm)
Cairo: 46 inches (117 cm)

Average yearly snowfall
Chicago: 38 inches (97 cm)
Cairo: 9 inches (23 cm)

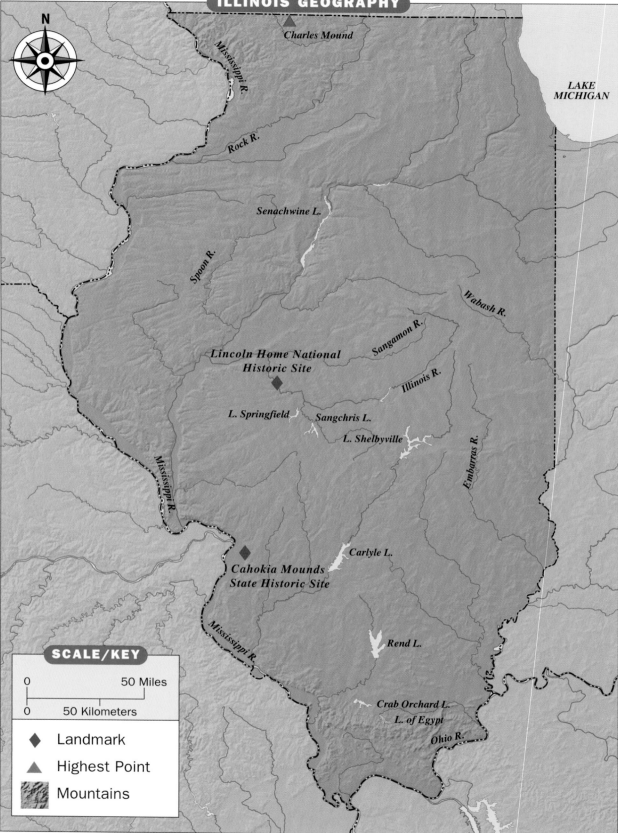

ILLINOIS GEOGRAPHY

N

▲ Charles Mound

LAKE MICHIGAN

Mississippi R.

Rock R.

Senachwine L.

Spoon R.

Wabash R.

Sangamon R.

Lincoln Home National Historic Site ◆

Illinois R.

L. Springfield

Sangchris L.

L. Shelbyville

Embarras R.

Mississippi R.

Carlyle L.

◆ Cahokia Mounds State Historic Site

Mississippi R.

Rend L.

Crab Orchard L.

L. of Egypt

Ohio R.

SCALE/KEY

```
0                    50 Miles
0          50 Kilometers
```

◆ Landmark

▲ Highest Point

Mountains

Windy City," is not directly related to the weather, but is an apt description. In the winter, ice-cold winds blow through the city.

From Prairies to Farmland

Illinois was originally prairie grasslands and forests. Mixed forests of oak, hickory, maple, beech, elm, and ash lined the streams and rivers. The land between these forests was covered in prairie grasses.

Settlers cleared most of the forests for fuel and timber and plowed the prairies to plant crops. Today a few isolated patches of prairie remain, but most of the state is given over to agriculture. Only about 10 percent of Illinois's original forests remain standing. About a quarter of this woodland comprises the Shawnee National Forest.

Wildlife

Bison, elk, wolves, bears, and mountain lions once roamed the prairies, forests, and hills of Illinois. By the time Illinois was admitted to the Union in 1818, these animals were nearly all gone.

The native white-tailed deer were virtually wiped out by the first decade of the twentieth century, but the State Department of Conservation began a program to restore the herds in 1933. The deer population has since grown rapidly.

Native bird species, including game birds such as quail and pheasant, are plentiful. Migratory bird populations explode in the spring and fall, as birds pass through the state by way of the Mississippi Valley.

Bullheads, carp, and catfish are plentiful in the streams and rivers of the state. Catfish are also raised commercially in areas once dug out for strip-mining coal.

Natural Resources

Illinois is rich in natural resources, particularly coal. Reserves of soft coal have been estimated at more than 100 billion tons. Petroleum is produced in the southern part of the state. Coal and petroleum together account for approximately two-thirds of the total value of mineral production in Illinois.

Another important mineral found in abundance in Illinois is fluorspar, which is used in the steel, chemical, and ceramics industries. Silica sand, used in the manufacture of glass bottles, is also an important natural resource.

Largest Lakes

Carlyle Lake
15 miles long (24 kilometers)
3.5 miles (5.6 km) wide
38 feet (11m) maximum depth

Rend Lake
13 miles (20.9 km) long
3 miles (4.8 km) wide
35 feet (10 m) maximum depth

Lake Shelbyville
20 miles (27 km) long
1.5 miles (2.4 km) wide
67 feet (20 km) maximum depth

Major Rivers

Mississippi River
2,350 miles (3,780 km) long
585 miles (941 km) along the Illinois border

Wabash River
475 miles (765 km) long

Spoon River
175 miles (281 km) long

Sangamon River
150 miles (241 km) long

Ohio River
140 miles (225 km) long

Transportation Cornerstone

> Hog Butcher for the World,
> Tool Maker, Stacker of Wheat,
> Player with Railroads and the Nation's Freight Handler;
> Stormy, husky, brawling,
> City of Big Shoulders.
>
> — *Carl Sandburg, "Chicago," 1914*

Illinois' diverse economy is led by transportation, agriculture, finance, and manufacturing, making the state fourth-ranked nationally in economic output. There are over six million people in Illinois' labor force. Illinoisans are among the most prosperous in the nation; they have the ninth highest per capita income in the United States. Many workers in Illinois belong to labor unions. That is hardly surprising, given that Illinois has a long history of union activity and labor organization. Some of the most important labor strikes and protests in the U.S. labor movement have taken place in Illinois.

Top Employers
(of workers age sixteen and over)

Services	33.0%
Retail and wholesale trade	21.0%
Manufacturing	19.0%
Government	12.0%
Finance, insurance and real estate	7.0%
Construction	5.0%
Agriculture	2.0%
Mining	0.3%

Illinois Gross State Product
Millions of dollars

Total gross state product $445,666

Finance, insurance & real estate $90,755

Manufacturing (includes printing & publishing) $72,563

Services $100,527

Mining $1,151

Agriculture, forestry, fishing, farms, agricultural services $3,575

Construction $20,059

Wholesale trade $35,342

Retail trade $36,683

Transportation & utilities $40,830

Government $44,180

Other $1

Source: U.S. Department of Commerce, Bureau of Economic Analysis, Regional Economic Analysis Division.

DID YOU KNOW?

In 1955 Ray Kroc, the founder of McDonald's Corporation, opened the first restaurant in the franchise in Des Plaines, Illinois. His profit that first day was $366.12.

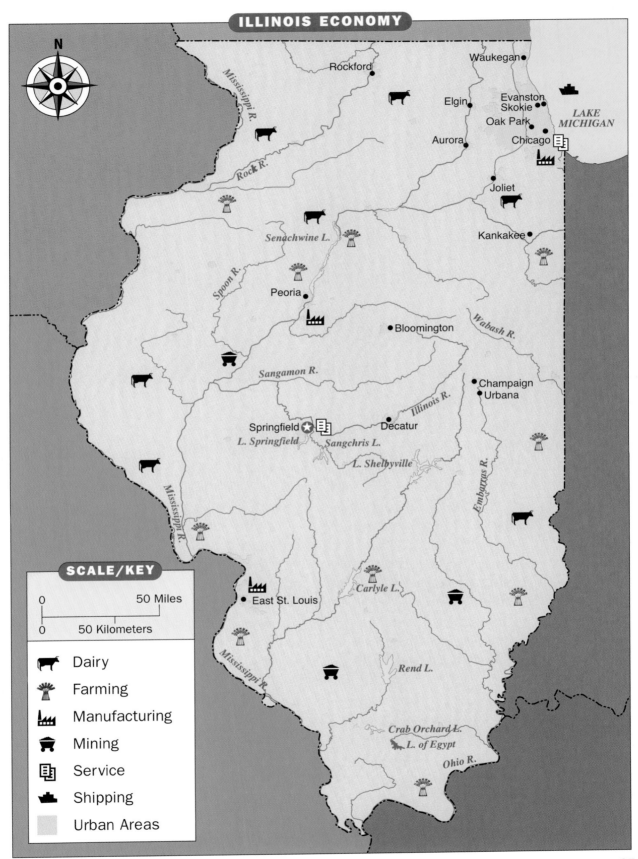

ILLINOIS ECONOMY

N

Rockford

Waukegan

Elgin

Evanston
Skokie
Oak Park

Aurora

Chicago

*LAKE
MICHIGAN*

Mississippi R.

Rock R.

Joliet

Kankakee

Senachwine L.

Spoon R.

Peoria

Bloomington

Wabash R.

Champaign
Urbana

Sangamon R.

Illinois R.

Springfield

Decatur

L. Springfield

Sangchris L.

L. Shelbyville

Embarras R.

Mississippi R.

SCALE/KEY

| 0 | 50 Miles |
| 0 | 50 Kilometers |

East St. Louis

Carlyle L.

Rend L.

Mississippi R.

Crab Orchard L.
L. of Egypt

Ohio R.

Key

- Dairy
- Farming
- Manufacturing
- Mining
- Service
- Shipping
- Urban Areas

Moving Around

Because of its central location and superior transportation system, Illinois is the sixth-largest U.S. exporter of goods — both domestically and internationally. With more than 2,000 miles (3,218 kilometers) of interstate highways and 34,500 miles (55,521 km) of state highways, the state provides a fast and efficient means of transporting materials by truck. Illinois boasts approximately 1,100 airports, landing areas, and heliports. Illinois's 1,118 miles (1,799 km) of navigable waterways, including the Illinois and Mississippi Rivers, also allow for the rapid flow of goods.

Chicago has the nation's second largest transportation system after New York City. Chicago is also both the national hub for Amtrak, the national passenger service railroad, and a key port city for ocean-going vessels. As a significant transportation center, Chicago is also favored nationally as a convention and meeting site.

Second only to New York City in the production of printed material, Chicago's publishing industry focuses on particular markets such as educational materials and encyclopedias. Chicago is also the home of many printing companies that serve publishers throughout the nation.

▲ *From left to right:* Corn is one of Illinois's key crops. The busy trading floor of the Chicago Stock Exchange.

DID YOU KNOW?

Each year Illinois produces 678 million gallons (3,082 liters) of ethanol — more than any other state — from 274 million bushels of Illinois corn.

▼ O'Hare International Airport in Chicago.

Tilling the Soil

More than 28 million acres (11,330,986 hectares) of land in Illinois — nearly 80 percent of the state's total land area — is used for farming. The state boasts about 76,000 farms, with an average size of 368 acres (149 ha). Illinois is one of the nation's leading producers of soybeans and corn. Given Illinois' climate and rich soil, a wide variety of crops are grown, including wheat. Illinois farms supply beef cows, dairy cows, and pigs to the national market.

The processing of farm crops and livestock is another major industry in Illinois. Some agricultural goods are processed into food, while others are ingredients for such consumer products as soap, wax, paper, and lumber.

▲ Beef cattle are an important part of the Illinois economy.

Finance

As the nation's oldest and most important commodities market, the Chicago Board of Trade is the centerpiece of the Illinois finance industry. On the floor of the Board of Trade, contracts are made and prices are set for agricultural products, including soybeans and corn, Illinois' two most important crops. The Chicago Stock Exchange and Chicago Mercantile Exchange are among the several exchanges in Illinois that trade company stocks.

Manufacturing

Steel plants established outside Chicago in the 1880s were among the first in the nation, and this industry is still going strong in Illinois, which is among the top five states in the production of raw steel. Illinois is also the home of many industries that turn raw steel into finished products. The state's steel supply and position as a major transportation center has made it especially suited to manufacturing large machinery, such as train cars and locomotives, printing presses, and agricultural equipment. In addition, Illinois is a national leader in the production of fabricated metals, rubber products, and electrical machinery.

Major Airports		
Airport	**Location**	**Passengers per year (approx)**
O'Hare International	Chicago	72,145,489
Midway	Chicago	12,681,966

Fastest-Growing Industries in Illinois
(based on number of job openings)

Personnel supply services

Eating and drinking places

Educational services

Miscellaneous business services

Nursing and personal care facilities

Management & public relations services

Hospitals

Computer and data processing services

Source: Northern Illinois Business and Industry Data Center at Northern Illinois State

Reform Pioneer

An Ordinance for the government of the Territory of the United States northwest of the River Ohio. Be it ordained by the United States in Congress assembled, That the said territory, for the purposes of temporary government, be one district, subject, however, to be divided into two districts, as future circumstances may, in the opinion of Congress, make it expedient.

— Northwest Ordinance, July 13, 1787

Carving Out a State

The Territory of Illinois became the twenty-first state in the Union on December 3, 1818. The state was carved out of the Northwest Territory, which became the official property of the new U.S. government at the close of the Revolutionary War. The U.S. government passed the Northwest Ordinances of 1784, 1785, and 1787, legislation that organized this territory and set the terms for statehood. Congress created the Illinois Territory in 1809, making the town of Kaskaskia its capital and Ninian Edwards governor. In 1818, with a population of 34,620, Illinois entered the Union. Shadrach Bond was the state's first governor. In 1820 the state capital moved from Kaskaskia to Vandalia. It moved once more in 1839 to Springfield, where it remains today.

The State Constitutions

Throughout Illinois's history, its legislature, known as the General Assembly, has been willing to draft new constitutions to address various social and political issues. The first state constitution allowed slave holders to keep their slaves but forbade new slaves from being brought into the state. In 1848 a new state constitution was passed, which abolished all slavery in Illinois. New constitutions were drafted again in 1870 and 1970. The 1970 constitution

Government Firsts

1979 — Jane Byrne was the first woman elected mayor of Chicago.

1983 — Harold Washington was the first African American elected mayor of Chicago.

expanded the Illinois Bill of Rights, outlawing discrimination based on race, creed, color, national ancestry, sex, or physical or mental handicap. It also relaxed residency rules, allowing more state citizens to vote, and made provisions for protecting the environment.

Pioneering Social Legislation

The Illinois state legislature has a long history of passing laws to protect the rights and well-being of workers, women, children, and the disadvantaged. In 1855 the state legislature established one of the first free public school systems in the nation. A state board of health was created in 1877. An 1883 law required that children must attend school for some part of the school year; 1893 legislation limited the number of hours children could work per week and also established factory inspections to improve working conditions.

In 1917 the Illinois state government was reorganized and made more efficient by bringing the more than one hundred independent commissions and agencies under the governor's control. With its emphasis on social and legislative reform, Illinois has been a model for other states around the country.

The State of the State

A governor, who can be elected to an unlimited number of four-year terms, leads the executive branch of the Illinois state government. Other top executives are the lieutenant governor, secretary of state, attorney general, treasurer, and comptroller, all also elected to four-year terms. The General Assembly is made up of two houses — the Senate with fifty-nine members and the House with one hundred eighteen members. Today power is fairly evenly split between Republicans and Democrats in the legislative branch of the Illinois government. The Illinois Supreme Court, with seven judges, has the final say in state judicial matters, with appellate, circuit, and claims courts throughout Illinois.

The Right to Vote

In 1891 the General Assembly gave women the right to vote in school elections. In 1913 it granted them the right to vote for presidential electors, the first state east of the Mississippi to allow women to vote in presidential elections. In 1920 it was the first to ratify the Nineteenth Amendment, which granted all female U.S. citizens the right to vote.

▼ The new state capitol building in Springfield opened in 1877.

Below the state government are three forms of local government: counties, townships, and municipalities. Illinoisans in the 102 counties in the state elect boards of commissioners to govern their affairs. Town meetings are still held in many areas. These were one of the earliest forms of government in colonial America, in which a town's eligible voters would meet to make decisions about how to govern themselves.

Presidential Politics

Two U.S. presidents and two first ladies — Abraham Lincoln, Ronald Reagan, Betty Ford, and Senator Hillary Rodham Clinton — have come from Illinois. When Reagan won the 1980 presidential election, among the opponents he defeated was fellow Illinoisan John Anderson, who ran on the Independent party ticket.

Illinois is an important state in presidential elections because of its large number of electoral votes. The Republican and Democratic parties battle over Illinois because it is a "swing state," meaning that no one can easily predict which party will win the state. Chicago is heavily Democratic, while suburban Chicago and north central Illinois are Republican. Voters in southern Illinois can go either way, so the presidential contest for Illinois is always close. In the 1960 presidential election, John F. Kennedy ran a close race against Richard M. Nixon. Kennedy's victory was secured when he won Illinois's electoral votes despite charges of vote fraud and corruption.

▲ Legislators conduct the business of the state inside the state capitol at Springfield.

Elected Posts in the Executive Branch		
Office	**Length of Term**	**Term Limits**
Governor	4 years	None
Lieutenant Governor	4 years	None
Secretary of State	4 years	None
Attorney General	4 years	None
Treasurer	4 years	None
Comptroller	4 years	None

The White House via Illinois

Two Illinoisans have served as president of the United States

ABRAHAM LINCOLN (1861–1865) Born in Hardin County, Kentucky, on February 12, 1809, Lincoln and his family moved from Kentucky to Indiana to settle in Illinois when Lincoln was twenty-one. Lincoln worked at many different occupations before being elected as Illinois state representative in 1834 for the first of four terms. He began practicing law in 1836 while serving in the state legislature and became one of the most respected lawyers in the state of Illinois. During his term in the U.S. House of Representatives (1847–49), Lincoln criticized U.S. involvement in the Mexican War, and his political career seemed to be over. Though he lost in his bid to defeat Stephen Douglas for a seat in the U.S. Senate in 1858, their debates brought him national attention. Lincoln's victory in the 1860 presidential election sparked the secession of southern states from the Union, and Lincoln had to deal with a nation on the brink of civil war. He faced a daunting task in bringing the Union back together. Lincoln led the nation through the Civil War with great political skill and compassion

and had high hopes for the future. However, he was assassinated just days after the South conceded defeat, and the task of repairing the Union fell to others. Remembered as the "Great Emancipator" of the slaves and as one of the nation's greatest presidents, Lincoln stands as one of the finest sons of Illinois.

RONALD REAGAN (1981–1989) Born in Tampico, Illinois, on February 6, 1911, Reagan's childhood was spent in Dixon, Illinois. After graduating from Eureka College in Illinois, Reagan began a career in radio broadcasting in the Midwest, and his broadcasts of Chicago Cubs baseball games became very popular. In 1937 he moved to California and began his career as a film actor. His involvement in politics began while working for an actor's union, and soon he was campaigning for other politicians. His 1966 election as governor of California was the beginning of a political rise that culminated in his victory in the 1980 presidential election. As president, Reagan cut taxes, increased military spending, and cut spending on social welfare programs. During his second term, relations with the Soviet Union improved, and Reagan remained an extremely popular president despite the eruption of a major scandal involving the illegal sale of weapons to foreign countries.

General Assembly			
House	**Number of Members**	**Length of Term**	**Term Limits**
Senate	59 senators	4 years	None
House of Representatives	118 representatives	2 years	None

Urban Thrills, Rural Charms

> . . . But Chicago is a great American City.
> Perhaps it is the last of
> the Great American cities
> — *Harriet Martineau, Society in America, 1837*

The third largest city in the nation, Chicago has rich offerings in entertainment and culture, from performing arts to museums to professional sports. Second City, the legendary improvisational comedy workshop, is a starting point for many of the nation's top comedians. The Steppenwolf Theater Company produces some of the most innovative work in American theater, as well as being a showcase for new artists.

Chicago boasts several first-rate museums. The Art Institute of Chicago features not only one of the world's finest collections of American and impressionist art, but also includes a prestigious school of art and design. The Field Museum of Natural History, an important research facility in anthropology and earth sciences, draws visitors with its famous dinosaur hall and exhibits of cultures from around the world. In addition to its permanent collection of African-American art and culture, the DuSable Museum of African-American History offers art festivals, workshops, and lectures all year long.

▼ The Art Institute of Chicago has held important exhibitions since its earliest days.

PICASSO

40 years of his art

FEB. 1 TO MAR. 3

THE ART INSTITUTE OF CHICAGO

EASY TO REACH — VERY LOW FARES — VIA
CHICAGO AURORA AND ELGIN RAILROAD
FAST, FREQUENT SERVICE

Making Music

When African Americans came to Chicago during the Great Migration, they introduced the city to the blues, imported from the Mississippi Delta. Before long, Chicago had its own version of the blues, which developed in the 1940s and 50s. Famous blues artists such as Buddy Guy, John Lee Hooker, and Willie Dixon all had their start in Chicago.

Art in Architecture

Modern architecture has an impressive showcase in Chicago. Visitors to the thirty-five-block area of downtown Chicago known as "the Loop" can travel up the observatory at the Sears Tower, the second-tallest building in the world as of 2001. A stroll through the Chicago neighborhood of Oak Park offers views of twenty-five buildings designed by Frank Lloyd Wright, one of the most important architects of the twentieth century.

Chicago takes full advantage of its lakefront setting, offering residents and visitors sandy beaches and an extensive park system right in the middle of the city. At the Chicago Botanic Garden in Glencoe, visitors can explore 385 acres (156 hectares) of gardens, prairies, and woodland areas. For thrill-seekers, north of Chicago near the Wisconsin border is Six Flags Great America, featuring live shows, themed landscapes, and death-defying rides, including a suspended spiral roller coaster.

▼ Illinois architect Frank Lloyd Wright became world-famous for innovative designs, such as the Dana-Thomas house in Springfield.

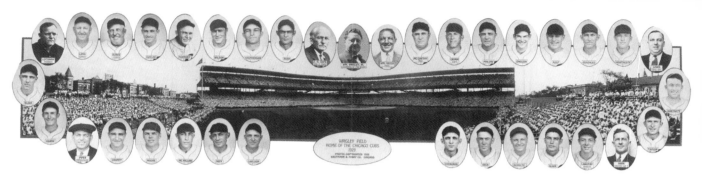

Sports

Team sports, whether at the college level, local
neighborhood leagues, or professional organizations, are an
important part of life in Illinois. The University of Illinois
has three major campuses, each with a wide selection of
sports teams. Football player Red Grange was a stand-out

Sport	Team	Home
Baseball	Chicago Cubs	Wrigley Field, Chicago
	Chicago White Sox	Comiskey Park, Chicago
Basketball	Chicago Bulls	United Center, Chicago
Football	Chicago Bears	Soldier Field, Chicago
Hockey	Chicago Blackhawks	United Center, Chicago
Soccer	Chicago Fire	Soldier Field, Chicago

▼ *Left to right:* Sears
Tower in Chicago is
the tallest building in
the United States;
Abraham Lincoln
served as a state
legislator in the old
state capitol building
in Springfield.

▲ The Chicago Bears take on the Green Bay Packers.

at the University of Illinois and then went on to play for the Chicago Bears in the 1920s and 1930s.

Chicago is home to professional sports teams in baseball, basketball, football, and hockey. Many star athletes have played in Illinois and made sports history — for example, basketball's Michael Jordan led the Chicago Bulls to six National Basketball Association (NBA) championships in 1991–1993 and 1996–1998.

Historic Sites

Illinois celebrates its rich history with many historic sites throughout the state. Black Hawk State Historic Park, located along the Rock River in northwestern Illinois, includes the Hauberg Indian Museum, dedicated to the culture of the Fox and Sauk Indians who lived in the area in the 1700s and 1800s. The park also features picnic areas, hiking and cross-country skiing trails, and a pioneer cemetery.

In western Illinois the Nauvoo Historic Site documents the Mormon community that settled here for a time in the 1800s. Visitors can see the reconstructed homes of Mormon leaders Joseph Smith and Brigham Young.

Illinois offers many attractions that honor Abraham Lincoln. The Lincoln Log Cabin site near Charleston, in south central Illinois, has a reconstruction of the last home of Lincoln's parents. Also on the grounds is a living history museum complete with a garden, orchard, smokehouse, and barn, to show visitors what life was like on a nineteenth-century farm. The state capital of Springfield is the location of Lincoln's tomb as well as a reconstruction of one of his law offices. Also in Springfield is the Old State Capitol building, the center of Illinois government from 1839 to 1876, where Lincoln served as a state legislator.

State and National Parks

Illinois has over one hundred state parks and wildlife areas, scattered throughout the state. The Mississippi, Illinois, and Ohio Rivers all offer opportunities for rafting and canoeing. Scenic areas for hiking, picnicking, or camping abound.

Mississippi Palisades State Park in northwestern Illinois offers spectacular views of the Mississippi from the steep cliffs rising up from the riverbanks. Fascinating rock formations, such as Indian Head and Twin Sisters, dot the landscape. Fishing on the Mississippi is also a popular pastime.

Located along the Illinois River, the Starved Rock State Park features dramatic sheer bluffs and stunning waterfalls.

▲ The Adler
Planetarium
in Chicago.

Visitors come here to enjoy hiking, horseback riding, and camping. Cave-in-Rock State Park, located near the Kentucky border on the Ohio River, is named for the 55-foot (17-km) wide cavern that was once the headquarters for bandits who preyed on unsuspecting travelers on the Ohio River. The area includes the historic town Cave-in-Rock.

Colleges and Universities

The Illinois state university system is composed of eight universities as well as the University of Illinois, which has three campuses in Chicago, Springfield, and Urbana-Champaign. More than fifty community colleges are also included. Many private colleges are located in Illinois, including the prestigious University of Chicago, a major center for education, scholarship, and research. With its highly respected and innovative education department, the university has had a significant impact on schools throughout the nation. Established in 1851, Northwestern University offers first-rate education with over twelve colleges and schools to choose from. Located in Evanston, Illinois, Northwestern is one of the nation's leading private universities, enrolling more than sixteen thousand students.

DID YOU KNOW?

More than seventy recipients of the Nobel Prize have been graduates and/or employees of the University of Chicago.

The Illinois State University System
(Total enrollment: more than 191,000 students)

Eastern Illinois University in Charleston

Chicago State University in Chicago

Governors State University in University Park

Illinois State University in Normal

Northeastern Illinois University in Chicago

Northern Illinois University in DeKalb

Southern Illinois University with campuses in Carbondale and Edwardsville and a medical school in Springfield

University of Illinois with campuses in Chicago, Springfield, and Urbana-Champaign

Western Illinois University in Macomb

Prairie State Pioneers

. . . we are each other's harvest;
we are each other's business;
we are each other's
magnitude and bond.
— Gwendolyn Brooks

Following are only a few of the thousands who lived, died, or spent most of their lives in Illinois while making extraordinary contributions to the state and the nation.

JANE ADDAMS
SOCIAL REFORMER
BORN: *September 6, 1860, Cedarville*
DIED: *May 21, 1935, Chicago*

Jane Addams was a reformer and pacifist who fought for the rights of workers, women, and children. She founded Hull House, one of the first social settlements in the United States. Addams lobbied the government for improved public health and sanitation, shorter workdays, and the banning of child labor. She also worked to secure the vote for women and for international peace. For her tireless efforts to improve housing, education, and working conditions across the nation, Addams received the Nobel Prize for Peace in 1931.

IDA B. WELLS-BARNETT
JOURNALIST AND REFORMER
BORN: *July 16, 1862, Holly Springs, MS*
DIED: *March 25, 1931, Chicago*

The daughter of slaves, Ida B. Wells became a journalist and an outspoken champion of civil rights. After friends were lynched by a mob, Wells began to organize groups dedicated to ending this violent practice. In 1895 Wells moved to Chicago and married attorney Ferdinand L. Barnett. Together, the couple published the Chicago *Conservator,* a newspaper that advocated civil rights. Wells published the first statistical report on lynching in 1895, *The Red Record.* In 1909 Wells was a member of the Committee of 40, who founded the National Association for the Advancement of Colored People. The NAACP fought to secure civil rights for African Americans. Wells once wrote, "One had better die fighting against injustice than die like a dog or a rat in a trap."

ROBERT ANDREWS MILLIKAN
PHYSICIST

BORN: *March 22, 1868, Morrison*
DIED: *December 19, 1953, San Marino, CA*

Robert Andrews Millikan was a physicist who did ground-breaking work on the elementary electronic charge. He left his position as full professor at the University of Chicago in 1921 to work at the California Institute of Technology (Cal Tech). While there, Millikan studied radiation from outer space, which he named cosmic rays. Millikan helped make Cal Tech one of the leading research universities in the nation. In 1923 he won the Nobel Prize for physics.

JACK BENNY
COMEDIAN AND ACTOR

BORN: *February 14, 1894, Waukegan*
DIED: *December 27, 1974, Beverly Hills, CA*

Jack Benny (born Benjamin Kubelsky) starred on radio and then television for over thirty years. From 1932 to 1955 *The Jack Benny Show* was one of the most popular radio broadcasts in the nation. Benny surrounded himself with a talented ensemble cast and the best comedy writers in the business, who often lampooned the comedian's frugality. In 1950 Benny made a successful transition to television when *The Jack Benny Show* began airing on the small screen.

ERNEST HEMINGWAY
WRITER AND SPORTSMAN

BORN: *July 21, 1899, Oak Park*
DIED: *July 2, 1961, Ketchum, ID*

Ernest Hemingway, one of the most important writers of the twentieth century, was famous for his simple, spare, and elegant writing style, which has influenced generations of writers. Among his most well-known works are *The Sun Also Rises* and *For Whom the Bell Tolls*. Hemingway drew upon his own experiences as a soldier and adventurer to craft some of his greatest works. A much-celebrated author, he was awarded the 1953 Pulitzer Prize for *The Old Man and the Sea* and the 1954 Nobel Prize. Hemingway committed suicide in 1961.

WALT DISNEY
ENTERTAINMENT PRODUCER

BORN: *December 5, 1901, Chicago*
DIED: *December 15, 1966, Los Angeles, CA*

Walt Disney created the beloved cartoon character Mickey Mouse and founded the motion picture and television studio and theme parks that bear his name. Disney was an animation pioneer who created a host of well-loved characters, including Donald Duck and Goofy. His first amusement park, Disneyland, opened in California in 1955. It was the first of many theme parks, which are visited by millions each year..

MARY ASTOR
ACTRESS

BORN: *May 3, 1906, Quincy*
DIED: *September 25, 1987, Woodland Hills, CA*

Mary Astor (born Lucille Vasconcellos Langharke) was a noted film and theater actress. Her film career began in 1921, during the silent film era. She was able to make the transition to talking films, thanks in part to her training as a stage actress. Perhaps Astor's most famous role was as co-star with Humphrey Bogart in *The Maltese Falcon* (1941). This Academy Award-winning actress overcame scandal in her personal life to enjoy a long career in film that lasted until the 1960s.

HARRY ANDREW BLACKMUN
SUPREME COURT JUSTICE

BORN: *November 12, 1908, Nashville*
DIED: *March 4, 1999, Arlington, VA*

Born in Illinois, Harry Blackmun grew up in St. Paul, Minnesota. A Harvard Law School graduate, he was nominated to the Supreme Court by President Richard Nixon in 1970 and unanimously confirmed by the Senate. Nixon had expected Blackmun to be a conservative judge, and for the first few years he was. In 1973, however, he surprised the world by writing a decision in the important case *Roe v. Wade* that pleased liberals. During the rest of his tenure on the Supreme Court, Blackmun wrote opinions and dissents that strongly supported the right to privacy, affirmative action, the separation of church and state, and the liberties of the first amendment.

GWENDOLYN ELIZABETH BROOKS
POET

BORN: *June 17, 1917, Topeka KS*
DIED: *December 3, 2000, Chicago*

Gwendolyn Brooks was one of the United States's most important poets. She was born in Kansas, but before she was a year old, her family moved to Chicago, where she lived for the rest of her life. Brooks wrote about the African-American community in which she lived, bringing the spirit of its people and the circumstances of their daily lives to national attention in her verse. She began publishing poems in the *Chicago Defender,* and published her first book, *A Street in Bronzeville,* in 1945. Five years later, she won the Pulitzer Prize for *Annie Allen,* a collection of poems about an African-American girl growing up in Chicago. In 1968 Brooks was made Poet Laureate of the State of Illinois, and from 1985 to 1986 served as Library of Congress consultant on poetry.

MILES DAVIS
JAZZ MUSICIAN

BORN: *May 26, 1926, Alton*
DIED: *September 28, 1991, Santa Monica, CA*

Miles Davis was a gifted trumpeter who had a profound influence on the evolution of jazz. He began playing the trumpet at age thirteen. Davis was a talented musician, bandleader, and composer who helped many musicians get their start by playing with him, including John Coltrane and Herbie Hancock. With his famous improvisational style, Davis was an innovator and one of the first jazz musicians to experiment with jazz-rock fusion.

BETTY FRIEDAN
WRITER AND ACTIVIST

BORN: *February 4, 1921, Peoria*

Betty Friedan is a feminist and author who was a leader in the women's rights movement in the 1960s and 1970s. In 1963 she published *The Feminine Mystique,* a ground-breaking book that explored women's subordination in modern society. Friedan co-founded the National Organization for Women (NOW), an organization dedicated to achieving equal rights for women. Friedan fought for the passage of the Equal Rights Amendment and protested against sex discrimination in the workplace and throughout American society.

MICHAEL JORDAN
BASKETBALL PLAYER

BORN: *February 17, 1963, Brooklyn, NY*

Generally considered the best all-around player in the history of professional basketball, Michael Jordan was drafted by the Chicago Bulls in 1984. He led the team to six NBA championships between 1991 and 1998. Jordan received numerous awards over the course of his NBA career, including Rookie of the Year and Most Valuable Player of the regular season and finals. He also led the U.S. basketball team to two Olympic gold medals. After the Bulls won the 1998 NBA championship, Jordan retired. Jordan came out of retirement in 2001 to join his new team, the Washington Wizards.

JIMMY CONNORS
TENNIS PLAYER

BORN: *September 2, 1952, East St. Louis*

Jimmy Connors won many tennis championships in the 1970s and 1980s. He learned to play the game from his mother and went on to become a top-ranked player. At the height of his career, he won major singles titles at Wimbledon, the U.S. Open, and the Australian Open. Known as a fierce competitor with a quick temper, Connors holds the all-time record for weeks ranked as the number-one professional tennis player — 273 weeks.

▼ Michael Jordan

Illinois

History At-A-Glance

1673
Louis Jolliet and Jacques Marquette arrive in Illinois.

1675
Marquette founds a mission with the Kaskaskia Indians.

1680
Robert La Salle establishes Fort Crevecoeur.

1763
France gives Illinois to Great Britain.

1778
George Rogers Clark gains control of Illinois for the rebel colonists.

1787
Final Northwest Ordinance is passed.

1818
Illinois becomes a state.

1825
Erie Canal opens.

1830
Abraham Lincoln moves to Illinois.

1832
Black Hawk War.

1839
Mormons found Nauvoo, Illinois; Springfield becomes state capital.

1848
Illinois and Michigan Canal is completed; the Chicago Board of Trade is established.

1600   **1700**   **1800**

1492
Christopher Columbus comes to New World.

1607
Capt. John Smith and three ships land on Virginia coast and start first English settlement in New World — Jamestown.

1754–63
French and Indian War.

1773
Boston Tea Party.

1776
Declaration of Independence adopted July 4.

1777
Articles of Confederation adopted by Continental Congress.

1787
U.S. Constitution written.

1812–14
War of 1812.

United States

History At-A-Glance

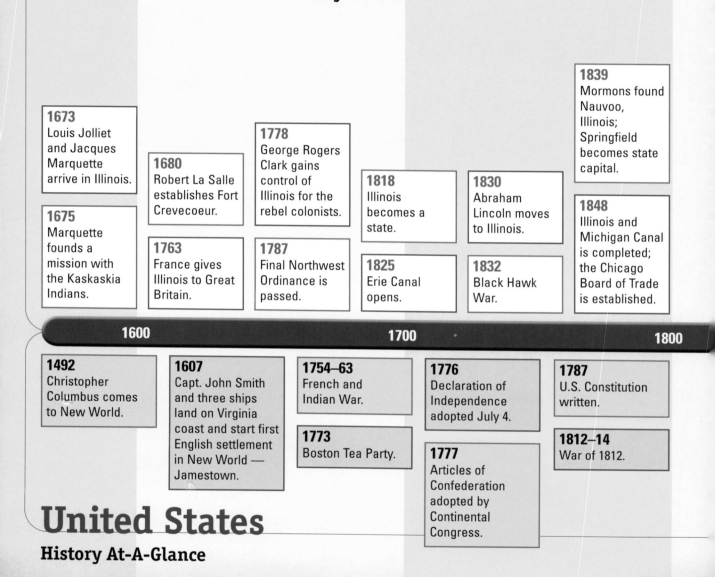

1858
Abraham Lincoln loses Senate battle with Stephen Douglas.

1860
Abraham Lincoln is elected president.

1871
Great Chicago Fire.

1885
The Home Insurance Building, the first skyscraper, is erected in Chicago.

1903
Illinois becomes the first state to establish an eight-hour work day.

1913
The General Assembly grants women the right to vote for presidential electors.

1920
Illinois is the first state to ratify the Nineteenth Amendment, granting all female U.S. citizens the right to vote in all elections.

1939
Oil is discovered in central and southern Illinois.

1942
Atomic chain reaction at University of Chicago.

1955–1976
Richard Daley serves as mayor of Chicago.

1970
Illinois holds its most recent constitutional convention.

1980
Ronald Reagan is elected president.

1800   **1900**   **2000**

1848
Gold discovered in California draws 80,000 prospectors in the 1849 Gold Rush.

1861–65
Civil War.

1869
Transcontinental Railroad completed.

1917–18
U.S. involvement in World War I.

1929
Stock market crash ushers in Great Depression.

1941–45
U.S. involvement in World War II.

1950–53
U.S. fights in the Korean War.

1964–73
U.S. involvement in Vietnam War.

2000
George W. Bush wins the closest presidential election in history.

2001
A terrorist attack in which four hijacked airliners crash into New York City's World Trade Center, the Pentagon, and farmland in western Pennsylvania leaves thousands dead or injured.

▼ **The 1909 Illinois State Fair.**

Festivals and Fun For All

Check web site for exact date and directions.

Chicago Asian-American Jazz Festival, Chicago

Music rooted in Asian traditions takes new form at this international celebration of jazz.

www.kzy.com/caajf

Chicago Blues Festival, Chicago

Chicago, a city known for its blues, hosts this popular music festival.

www.ci.chi.il.us/SpecialEvents/Festivals/Blues2001

Chicagoland Boat Show, Chicago

A four-day show featuring every type of water craft.

www.lemta.com/boatshows/chicagoland

Decatur Celebration, Decatur

Illinois's largest free family street festival features national entertainment, dozens of street attractions, fourteen show stages, and more, that line twenty-two city blocks.

www.decaturcelebration.com

Chicago Botanic Garden Art Festival, Chicago

One hundred artists and their art are featured at this fabulous festival.

www.amdurproductions.com/botanic

Insect Fear Film Festival, Urbana

Afraid of bugs? Then this film festival isn't for you. Sponsored by the University of Illinois, the festival features films starring all sorts of creepy-crawlies.

www.life.uiuc.edu/entomology/ifff.html

Gebhard Woods Dulcimer Festival, Morris

A festival celebrating the American folk instrument, the dulcimer.

http://gwdf.org

Great Grafton Tow Boat Festival, Grafton

Tour the Mississippi and Illinois Rivers aboard the Anastasia.

altonriverboats.com/grafton.htm

Illinois State Fair, Springfield

For nearly 150 years the Illinois State Fair has showcased the state's agricultural history while providing a rollicking good time.

www.state.il.us/fair

Southern Illinois Festival of Irish Music and Dance, Carbondale

Art, music, film, dance, and more!
intranet.siu.edu/~irish

Ravinia Festival, Ravinia

A nationally recognized performing arts festival.
www.ravinia.org

University of Chicago Folk Festival of Traditional Music, Chicago

One of the longest-running, college-sponsored folk festivals in the nation celebrates folk music from around the world.
www.uofcfolk.org/index.html

The Classic Balloon Festival, Danville

Fly high over Illinois at this balloon festival.
www.balloonlife.com/publications/
balloon_life/9708/danville.htm

Books

Altman, Linda Jacobs. *The Pullman Strike of 1894: Turning Point for American Labor.* Brookfield, CT: Millbrook Press, 1994. Read about the strike that brought transportation to a halt in 1894.

Bial, Raymond. *Where Lincoln Walked.* New York: Walker & Co., 1998. Learn about Lincoln's life before he became president and see pictures of the world in which he grew up.

Murphy, Jim. *The Great Fire.* New York: Scholastic, 1995. Find out about the fire that destroyed much of Chicago in 1871.

Sammartino McPherson, Stephanie. *Peace and Bread: The Story of Jane Addams.* Minneapolis: Carolrhoda Books, 1993. A book about a remarkable Illinoisan who dedicated her life to others and won the Nobel Peace Prize.

Sayre, April Pulley. *Grassland.* New York: Twenty First Century Books, 1995. Discover more about the natural environment in Illinois.

Wills, Charles A. *A Historical Album of Illinois.* Brookfield, CT: Millbrook Press, 1994. A thorough history of Illinois from before Europeans arrived up to the present day.

Web Sites

▶ Official state web site
www.state.il.us

▶ Official state capital web site
www.springfield.il.us

▶ Official Chicago web site
www.ci.chi.il.us

▶ Illinois State Historical Society
www.historyillinois.org

Films

Grubin, David. *The Time of the Lincolns.* Boston, MA: David Grubin Productions, Inc./The American Experience/WGBH, 2001. The private and public life of the nation's sixteenth president, Illinoisan Abraham Lincoln.

King, George. *Goin' to Chicago.* San Francisco, CA: California Newsreel, 1994. Hear the stories of African Americans who migrated from hardship in the South to build a vibrant community in Chicago's Bronzeville.

INDEX

Note: Page numbers in *italics* refer to illustrations or photographs.

A

Abraham Lincoln's Home and Burial Site, 7
Addams, Jane, 4, 14, 38
Adler Planetarium, *37*
African Americans, 7, 15, 19, 28, 32
age distribution, 16
agriculture, 4, 13, 23, *26*, 27
airports, 26, 27
Algonquian language, 8
Amish community, *19*
Anderson, John, 30
architecture, 14, 29, 33, 33
area of Illinois, 6, 20
Art Institute of Chicago, 4, 32, 32
Astor, Mary, 40
atomic bomb, 15
attractions
  architecture, *14*, 29, 33, *33*
  arts and culture, 32
  festivals, 44–45
  lakes of Illinois, 4, 7, 12, 21, 23
  music, 4, 33, 40–41
  rivers, 8, 12, *17*, 21, 23, 36
  sports, 34–35, 41
Auditorium Theatre, 14
Aurora, 6

B

baseball, 34
basketball, 34–35
Benny, Jack, 39
bird (state), 6
Black Hawk, 11, *11*
Black Hawk State Historic Park, 35
Blackmun, Harry Andrew, 40
blues, 33
Bond, Shadrach, 28
books about Illinois, 45
Brooks, Gwendolyn Elizabeth, 40
burial mounds, 8, 9, 21
Burnham, Daniel H., 14
Byrne, Jane, *28*

C

Cahokia Indians, *8*, 9
Cahokia Mounds State Historic Park, 7, *9*
capitals of Illinois, 6, 28
capitol building, *29*, *34*, 36
Carlyle Lake, 23
Carson Pirie Scott and Company Building, *14*

cattle industry, 27
Cave-in-Rock State Park, 37
Chamberlain, Everett, 13
Charles Mound, 21
Chicago, 4, 6, 7, 13, *17*, *20*, *36*
Chicago & Alton Railroad Company, 12
Chicago Asian-American Jazz Festival, 44
Chicago Bears, 34–35, *35*
Chicago Blackhawks, 34
Chicago Blues Festival, 44
Chicago Board of Trade, 12
Chicago Botanic Garden, 33
Chicago Botanic Garden Art Festival, 44
Chicago Bulls, 34
Chicago Cubs, 34
Chicago Daily News, *33*
Chicago Fire, 34
Chicago O'Hare Airport, 7, *26*, 27
Chicago River, *17*, 21
"Chicago School" of architecture, *14*
Chicago Stock Exchange, *26*
Chicago White Sox, 34
Chicagoland Boat Festival, 44
Church of Jesus Christ of Latter-day Saints, 10–11, 35
cities of Illinois, *5*, 6
civil rights movement, 38–39
Civil War, 12
Clark, George Rogers, 9
Classic Balloon Festival, The, 45
Cleveland, Grover, 14
climate, 21–23
Clinton, Hillary Rodham, 30
Colbert, Elias, 13
Connors, Jimmy, 41
Conservator, 38
constitutions, 28–29
corn, 26, 26

D

Daley, Richard J., 15
Dana-Thomas House, 33
dance (state), 6
Davis, Miles, 40–41
Decatur Celebration, 44
Democratic Party, 15
Dimiceli, Sal, 18
Disney, Walt, 39
Douglas, Stephen, 11
DuSable Museum of African-American History, 32

E

economy and commerce
  agriculture, 4, 13, 23, *26*, 27
  airports, 26, 27
  cattle industry, 27
  Chicago Stock Exchange, *26*
  employers, 24
  exports, 26
  finance industry, 27
  fur trade, 8–9
  gross state product, 24
  industries, 12–13, 27
  labor force and conflicts, 14, 24
  mail-order retail business, 13, *13*
  manufacturing, 27
  natural resources, 23, 25
  oil industry, 14–15, 23
  per capita income, 24
  publishing industry, 26
  transportation, 5, 12–13, 14, 26
education of Illinois residents, 7, 15, *16*, *18*, 37
Edwards, Ninian, 28
employers, 24
Erie Canal, 12
ethanol production, 26
ethnic makeup of Illinois, 16–19
executive branch, 29, 30
exports, 26

F

farming, 4, 13, 23, 26, 27
Feminine Mystique, The, (Friedan), 41
Fermi, Enrico, 15
festivals, 44–45
Field Museum of Natural History, 32
films about Illinois, 45
finance industry, 27
fish (state), 6
flower (state), 6
fluorspar, 23
football, 34–35
Ford, Betty, 30
Fort Crevecoeur, 8
fossil (state), 6
Fox Indians, 8, 11, 35
French and Indian War, 8–9
Friedan, Betty, 41
fur trade, 8–9

G

game animal (state), 6
Gebhard Woods Dulcimer Festival, 44

General Assembly, 29, *31*
geography of Illinois, 20–23, 22
geology, 21
German community, 18
government. See politics and political figures
Gray, Hannah, 7
Great Chicago Fire of 1871, 13, *14–15*
Great Depression, 14
Great Grafton Tow Boat Festival, 44
Great Lakes, 12
Great Migration, 19, 33
gross state product, 24

H

Hamburger University, 7
Hauberg Indian Museum, 35
Haymarket Square strike, 14
Hemingway, Ernest, 39
highway system, 5, 26
historic sites, 35–36
hockey, 34
Home Insurance Building, 7, 13, 14
House of Representatives, 29
Hudson River, 12
Hull House, 38

I

Illiniwek, 8
Illinois & Michigan Canal, 12
Illinois Bill of Rights, 29
Illinois River, 36
Illinois State Fair, *42–43*, 44
Illinois State University System, 37
Illinois Supreme Court, 29
Illinois Territory, 28
immigration, 16–19
income, 24
industries in Illinois, 12–13, 27
Insect Fear Film Festival, 44
insect (state), 6
Irish community, 18

J

jazz, 4, 40–41
Jenny, William LeBaron, 13, *14*
Jolliet, Louis, 8
Jordan, Michael, 41, 41
judicial branch, 29

K

Kaskaskia, 28
Kaskaskia Indians, 8, *8*, 9
Kennedy, John F., 30
Kroc, Ray, 24

L

labor force and conflicts, 14, 24
Lake Michigan, 4, 7, 21
Lake Shelbyville, 23
lakes of Illinois, 4, 7, 12, 21, 23
LaSalle, Robert, 8
latitude, 20
legislative branch, 30
Lincoln, Abraham, 7–8, 11–12, *12*, 30, *31*, 35
Lincoln Log Cabin, 35
Lincoln Park, 36

M

mail-order retail business, 13, 13
Manhattan Project, 15
manufacturing, 27
maps of Illinois, 5, 22, 25
Marquette, Jacques, 8
McDonald's corporation, 7
Michigamea Indians, 8
Middle Mississippi Indians, 8
Midway Airport, 27
Millikan, Robert Andrews, 39
mineral (state), 6
Mississippi Palisades State Park, 36
Mississippi River, 8, 21, 23, 36
Monk's Mound, 8
Mormon community, 10–11, 35
Moseley-Braun, Carol, 7, 15
motto (state), 6
mounds, 9, 21
Museum of Science and Industry, 7
music, 4, 33, 40–41

N

name of Illinois, 4, *8*, 20
National Association for the Advancement of Colored People (NAACP), 38
Native Americans, 7–8, *8*, 9
natural resources, 23
Nauvoo Historic Site, 35
New Salem, *21*
nickname of Illinois, 4, *8*, 20
Nineteenth Amendment, 7, 29
Nixon, Richard M., 30
Nobel Prize, 37, 38
Northwest Ordinance, 10, 28
Northwest Territory, 10, 28
Northwestern University, 37

O

O'Hare International Airport, 7, *26*, 27
Ohio River, 23, 36
oil industry, 14–15, 23
Ozark Mountains, 21

P

Peoria, 6
Peoria Indians, 8, 8
per capita income, 24
petroleum, 23
politics and political figures
  Addams, Jane, 4, 14, 38
  Anderson, John, 30
  Blackmun, Harry Andrew, 40
  branches of government, 29–30
  Byrne, Jane, 28
  Cleveland, Grover, 14
  Clinton, Hillary Rodham, 30
  Daley, Richard J., 15
  Douglas, Stephen, 11
  Friedan, Betty, 41
  Kennedy, John F., 30
  Lincoln, Abraham 8, 11–12, *12*, 30, 31, 35
  Moseley-Braun, Carol, 7, *15*
  Nixon, Richard M., 30
  Reagan, Ronald, 15, 30, 31
  Washington, Harold, 28
Pope, Nathaniel, 7
population, 6, 16–17
prairie land, 20, 23
presidents from Illinois, 30
Proclamation Line of 1763, 9
protests, 24
publishing industry, 26

R

railroads, 12–13, 14
rainfall, 21
Ravinia Festival, 45
Reagan, Ronald, *15*, 30, *31*
Red Record, The, 38
religion, 10–11, 19, 35
Rend Lake, 23
reservoirs, 23
Revolutionary War, 9
Ridgeway, R., 20
rivers, 8, 12, 17, 21, 23, 36
Rockford, Illinois, 6
rural areas, 19

S

St. Lawrence Seaway, 4
Sandburg, Carl, *33*
Sangamon River, 23
Sauk Indians, *8, 11*, 35
seal of Illinois, 28
Sears Roebuck and Company, 13
Sears Tower, 7, 33, *34*
Shawnee Hills, 21
Shawnee National Forest, 21
Six Flags Great American, 33
size of Illinois, 20

skyscrapers, 7, 13, 33, *34*
slavery, 10
Smith, Joseph, 10–11, 35
snowfall, *21*
soccer, 34
social legislation, 29
song (state), 6
Southern Illinois Festival of Irish Music and Dance, 45
Spoon River, 23
sports, 34–35, 41
Springfield, 6, 28, 29
Starved Rock State Park, *21*, 36
statehood, 6, 10, 28
Steppenwolf Theater Company, 32
stock exchange, *26*
Sullivan, Louis, *14*

T

Tamaroa Indians, 8, *8*
temperature, *21*
Time Is Now, The, (nonprofit organization), 18
timeline of Illinois history, 42–43
topography, 21
transportation, 5, 12–13, 14, 26
tree (state), 6
Twain, Mark, 16

U

University of Chicago, 15
University of Chicago Folk Festival of Traditional Music, 45
University of Illinois, 37
urban areas, 19. *See also* Chicago, Illinois; specific cities

V

Vandalia, 28

W

Wabash River, 23
Ward, Aaron Montgomery, 13
Washington, Harold, 28
waterways of Illinois, 5
web sites about Illinois, 45
Wells-Barnett, Ida B., 38–39
wildlife, *20*, 23
World War I, 14
World War II, 15
Wright, Frank Lloyd, 33

Y

Young, Brigham, 11, 35